79 Ways
Calm A
Crying Baby

DIANA S. GREENE

ILLUSTRATIONS BY ROBERT MANSFIELD

POCKET BOOKS

New York   London   Toronto   Sydney   Tokyo   Singapore

This book was written by two parents based on their own
experiences, those of their friends, and research of medical
and parenting literature. If you know or suspect that your
child's crying has a physical or psychological cause, you
should consult a physician or qualified health professional.

An *Original* publication of POCKET BOOKS

POCKET BOOKS, a division of Simon & Schuster Inc.
1230 Avenue of the Americas, New York, NY 10020

ISBN: 0-671-66247-3

First Pocket Books trade paperback printing November 1988

10 9 8 7 6 5 4

POCKET and colophon are trademarks
of Simon & Schuster Inc.

Printed in the U.S.A.

To Marissa,
who made this all possible,
and impossible.

*Thanks to all those parents, too numerous to
mention, whose many ideas enriched this book.
Thanks also to Elaine Pfefferblit for her faith and
support, and in memory of Frank Schwartz,
whose help will always be remembered.*

Contents

SECTION SIX: MISCELLANEOUS, OR EVERYTHING ELSE, INCLUDING THE KITCHEN SINK 121

Preface

We began parenting with starry-eyed optimism. Our image of child care was doing housework and reading as our serene child spent most of her waking hours peacefully gazing at mobiles, playing with a rattle, gumming her lips, or engaging in some other captivating activity. We even entertained the absurdly naive notion that one of us could watch her at the office, slipping her a bottle now and then as needed, while the other went off to class for an hour or two. We quickly learned the hard reality of the life of a parent.

All babies cry. Perfect babies (of which there are only a few) cry only when they are tired or hungry. Real babies (the vast majority) cry for unknown reasons. This book is for parents, grandparents, and other caretakers of real babies. If you believe the conventional wisdom that all you can do is feed, burp, change, hold, and rock an infant, you are missing a great treasure of unusual ways to calm a crying baby.

We stumbled across this fact two and one-half weeks into our parenting career as we were vacuuming the house. Our friends from Atlanta, John and Tina, were arriving that evening, our first post-partum guests, and we were desperately trying to clean. Finally we were forced to lay down our daughter and ignore her cries for a few minutes. When we turned on the vacuum cleaner, instead of escalating into hysteria, she became completely quiet and closed her eyes. Intrigued, we turned off the vacuum and she began to cry. On again, quiet, off again, cry—it was like magic.

We were anxious to impress our childless friends with how serene and angelic a newborn can be, but as soon as we returned from the airport, she became unconsolably hysterical. She wouldn't take the breast; walking outside, rocking, holding, nothing would work. Suddenly, we seized on the inspiration of turning on the vacuum. Once again, it worked like magic.

If something as improbable as the unpleasant blaring of a vacuum cleaner worked so automatically, who knew what else? The possibilities were endless. We set about experimenting with all manner of bizarre and imaginative techniques. Fortunately for us, our daughter gave us plenty of opportunity to do so over the following months.

This book catalogues what we came up with, as well as ideas we learned from talking with parents of similarly afflicted infants. We present what worked for us and others in the hope that these ideas will expand your repertoire of quieting tricks. (We don't mention the experiments that failed, like the attempt to keep her pacifier from falling out by tying rubber bands to the handle and hooking them around her ears). But before we get into all of that, you had best learn something about why babies cry, and why you should try to calm them.

Diana S. Greene and Mark A. Hall
(Mom and Dad)
Tempe, Arizona, 1988

Introduction

FACTS ABOUT CRYING

THE NATURE OF THE BEAST. This book deals with fussy babies under the age of one, those newborns who cry when there is no obvious reason. Some parents and doctors call this "colic," but using a special medical term can be misleading. Thinking in terms of a medical problem may help some parents to cope with the extreme difficulty of dealing with a very fussy baby. If so, that is fine, but the best guess is that there is no specific physical cause for excessive crying. Therefore, it is best to speak in ordinary terms: there are easy babies, fussers, very difficult babies, and a few extremely trying ones.

SILVER LINING. Crying, far from being an illness, has a number of advantages that are helpful to keep in mind during the most difficult times. Penelope Leach, a well-known British child care author, tells the story of a first-time mom whose dehydrated and malnourished baby had to be hospitalized because it never demanded anything. At least this won't happen to your fussy child. It has been said

5

that fussy babies are more intelligent. There is no proof of this, but we think that they do have the potential to develop faster because their fussiness demands more attention and therefore they become more interactive. Some fussers (like ours) tend to sleep better from all the physical exertion. And criers have a significantly lower incidence of SIDS (crib) deaths.

HOW MANY AND HOW OFTEN. The human cry is one of nature's loudest sounds. At eighty to eighty-five decibels, it is as loud as an unmuffled truck, not far below the pain threshold. It is understandable, then, that parents of fussy kids tend to see nothing but a sea of tranquillity outside their home. They wonder why God has punished them if there are so many other perfectly calm kids around. This false impression results from two facts of nature: Babies quickly grow out of the fussiest period after the first few months, and they are fussiest when they are at home alone with their parents. Various studies have identified a substantial number of fussers among our midst. (You too may have been one.) Researchers say that one-fourth to one-half of babies are fussy, with some one-half of those being very difficult (what might be called colicky). With over three and one-half million births each year, that makes for a lot of noise pollution.

How much do "normal" and "colicky" babies cry? No one really knows. Some researchers say normal babies cry only a few minutes per day; others say as much as two and one-half hours is average. The findings for fussy babies range from one to three hours. The problem with these studies is that the amount of crying varies widely depending on how parents respond to their children. One thing we do learn from these studies is that uncontrollable crying tends to follow a typical pattern in the first few months. The reason you often hear of the "three-month colic" is that, for most (but not all) fussy babies, heavy crying begins at about two weeks, increases to a crescendo at six to eight weeks, and comes back down to manageable levels around three to four months.

The most important fact we learn from these studies though is what some parents learn only through brute experience: Responding to crying in a variety of different ways dramatically decreases the amount of crying. In a 1984 study published by *Pediatrics,* Dr. Bruce Taubman showed that counseling parents on more effective responses to crying reduced crying in fussy babies by seventy percent, down to the same level as the average baby!! So the most important question to ask is not what starts the crying but what will stop it.

CAUSES AND CURES. Nevertheless, we all have a natural human instinct to seek some understanding of our misery. You can spend countless hours discussing, debating, researching, and arguing about the cause of your daughter's excessive crying. The only solid conclusion is that no one can know the mind of another. For instance, suppose a baby stops crying when she is given her mother's breast. Does this prove that she was hungry? Not necessarily. It is equally likely that she was crying for some other reason and was pacified by the warmth and comfort of breast-feeding. It is obvious that a child with a scraped knee who stops crying when given a lollipop isn't suffering from a sugar deficiency, but the point is less obvious with a helpless, nonverbal infant.

In dealing with a newborn, the lesson is that the cause of crying is less important than the cure. The goal is not to understand the why but the how. Yet, it is difficult to cope without some understanding of why this unmuffled truck is suddenly parked in your life, so here are some theories.

THREE STAGES OF GROWTH

Think of a baby as growing through three stages: (1) newborn infant; (2) older infant and (3) toddler. These correspond roughly to zero to six months, six to twelve months, twelve to eighteen months. During early infancy, cries are entirely instinctive, that is, based on needs, temperament, or inborn personality. Some babies are just more demanding, less tolerant than others, or perhaps it's better to think of these kids as active rather than passive, extroverted rather than introverted.

PARADISE LOST. But what triggers the crying? Of what are they intolerant? Well, imagine yourself in a warm, comforting cosmic embrace where your every need is met. Now, think of the real world. Notice any differences? Don't you think you might also be a little bit put off by the rude abruptness of birth? Not to mention that your constant supply of nourishment has been cut off. In the words of one psychologist, birth "represents a loss of paradise, the interruption of the pleasurable primal state." The wonder is that babies don't cry all the time.

Viewing the cause of crying as any departure from the nirvana of the womb helps to maintain a more understanding attitude about your unmuffled truck. This also explains why those calming techniques that duplicate conditions of the womb work well.

COMMUNICATION AND KNOWLEDGE. During the second phase of older infancy, crying becomes a learned response. As baby begins to develop some awareness of her environment, crying is her first tool of communication, indeed, her only means of interaction with the outside world. Crying during this phase becomes her first expression of knowledge and recognition: "I know I want something and I know there is someone out there who can provide it."

9

But, again, what is the "it," if not food, sleep, or warmth? Once again, no one knows. Minor and major needs both result in crying because this is the only means of communication. Maybe all he wants is companionship and stimulation. Maybe it's an elemental sense of boredom or frustration in being aware of things but not being able to interact with them. If so, this explains why so many calming techniques relate to stimulation.

You will often be puzzled by the unpredictability of fussy spells during the first year. Kids will be horrible for a few days, then perfectly serene for several more. Just when you think you have found a permanent solution or have passed that much-anticipated three-month watershed, a new round will start. These may be subtle developmental phases. As baby acquires and masters new skills such as reaching, holding, sitting, standing, etc., he passes from the frustration of being aware of a new distant horizon to the gratification of reaching it. Just as he experiences the boredom of mastery, he becomes aware of a new horizon and so the frustration begins again. Viewed in this light, fussy spells are a welcome signal because, like the rings of a tree trunk, they mark your child's growth.

WHERE THIS BOOK STOPS. The third phase of crying begins with toddlerhood, roughly when speaking begins. This is the age of emotional crying, temper tantrums, and power struggles. The toddler has learned other ways to express her needs, and crying is no longer the sole means of communication. This phase introduces a whole new set of problems that are not dealt with in this book.

The clearest idea to keep in mind about the cause of crying is that, usually, there is no particular or troubling cause. Crying is fundamental to every baby's basic makeup, not solely a call of distress. During early infancy, it is an instinctive response to any unpleasant feeling, virtually the only response a newborn has. During later infancy, it is the only tool for communication, so it serves to signal both distress and minor annoyances. As is true for adults, annoyances come from limitless sources, life in general, and the world at large. The difference is that babies can't sort through these annoyances and deal with them. That is why they have parents to comfort them.

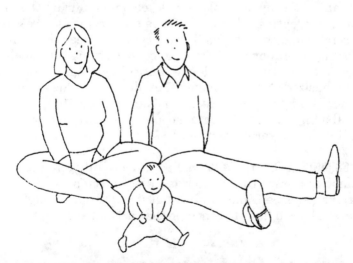

THE SPOILING MYTH

THE HOUSEHOLD TYRANT. In the 1920s and 1930s, U.S. government publications advised mothers that picking up a fussy baby taught him "that crying will get him what he wants, sufficient to make a spoiled, fussy baby, and a household tyrant whose continual demands make a slave of the mother." As late as 1962, a prominent pediatrician reported in a leading medical journal that two to three hours of crying per day was "normal," healthy, and necessary, and that efforts to avoid the inevitable would only lead to trouble.

This is a dangerous view. The most serious threat to your infant's healthy psychological development during the first year is adopting the rigid attitude that crying is necessary exercise and that responding to crying will lead to spoiling. Precisely the opposite is true. Excessive crying is unhealthy, and *refusing* to respond is the *cause* of spoiling! It cannot be emphasized strongly enough that, during the first year of life, calming infants presents no danger of spoiling. The real danger is that by not responding, you will create a child with a warped personality.

RESPONDING IS NOT SPOILING. Spoiling is a difficult and emotional issue that divides families and creates tremendous personal conflict, but if you think through it carefully, you have to conclude that it is impossible to spoil a child during the first year by responding too much. First, consider what it means to be spoiled. A spoiled infant would be one who uses crying as a manipulative control technique, in other words, simply as a means to exercise power over his parents, not to obtain something he wants. This requires a rather sophisticated level of intellectual development, a level that is not possible until he begins to talk. By this age, your child will have other means of communication than crying, so you will be better able to tell when his cries represent true need or only purposeful manipulation.

Let's go back to the three stages of growth. At birth, crying represents either pure instinct or simple communication. Infants are not aware of themselves or their environment in any meaningful sense. Life consists of a bombardment of disorganized sensory stimulation and instinctive response. The only response newborns are capable of is crying. If your child cries, it must be due to some unpleasant stimulus. Not responding is cruel. Responding cannot spoil him because he cannot associate his cry with your response; he is not even aware of who you are and who he is.

By around six months, however, babies begin to use crying as a learned behavior. They know that the way to get what they want is to cry. But this still is not spoiling. It is teaching. Crying is how your child first explores the outside world. It is his only means of communication. Not responding is like taking him out of school.

The problem is that older babies cry equally for minor annoyances and major distresses. Everything from boredom or an itch to serious hunger and tiredness tends to produce the same reaction. Reinforcing this behavior can lead to developing bad habits. But these habits are not the same as spoiling because they are not permanent psychological traits. They can be broken rather easily.

At around six to nine months, it is appropriate for parents to begin to teach very clear rules about when crying will work and when it won't. For instance, during the second half of the year, most parents make a point of not responding in the middle of the night except for serious distress such as night terrors or illness. But these rules must be clear enough for your baby to understand, as clear as night and day. It won't work to not respond when you are tired, or after 4:00 P.M., or on Tuesdays and Thursdays. Unless the logic of your rules is very clear, they will only confuse and cause more cries.

GUIDELINES FOR RESPONDING. The key to the spoiling question, then, is understanding which stage of development your child is in. Failing to distinguish these various mental stages is probably the cause of much of the confusion and conflicting advice over spoiling. Well-intentioned grandparents may have only foggy, distant memories of parenting. They tend to apply to infants rules that are appropriate only for children. New parents affected with the idyllic image of newborn serenity doubt their own instincts and skills when confronted with an unconsolable child and so they are susceptible to suggestions that they are doing something wrong. Parents need to keep in mind a strong vision of these guidelines:

During the early months when an infant's cries are purely instinctive, there is absolutely no harm in picking him up. This does not mean you must hold him every second of the day. No permanent harm will come from setting him down to cry when this is necessary to meet other demands. But it does mean that it is safe to err on the side of excessive holding. During the second stage, when you begin to sense that your baby is crying purposefully, you should begin to set some basic rules about when you will respond and when you won't, but again there is no real harm in excess, because he is crying essentially out of habit, not out of conscious awareness of his ability to control you. The third stage begins only when the child has more than primitive reasoning powers. Only then does the true power to manipulate, which is the mark of a spoiled child, become possible. But by then, you will have had plenty of time to modify any bad habits.

INTUITION. The strongest evidence against the spoiling myth is a parent's—particularly a mother's—natural impulse to respond to cries. Mothers have amazing sensitivity to their babies' cries. They can pick them out of a crowd of seemingly indistinguishable wails. Many breast-feeding mothers immediately begin to let down milk when their children call out. They are woken out of a dead sleep by faint whimpers. In short, they experience an over-whelming physical and emotional compulsion to respond.

It doesn't take a Charles Darwin to realize that we are intended to respond to our children. Why would nature

have provided so thoroughly for an innate behavior if it were harmful? As in all other areas of biology, innate characteristics evolve to serve a need. Because humans are the only animals that cry with such determination, it is likely that the need is some uniquely human one. The most obvious and likely candidate is intellectual and emotional development.

Crying and parental response create what scientists have called an "interactive dyad," that is, a give-and-take relationship between baby and parent. A baby's cries begin instinctively. A mother's response reinforces the instinct. The baby gradually becomes aware of the relationship between the cry and the response. In other words, she begins to learn. The cry then becomes a learned form of communication which continues to produce a parental response, giving her a sense of control over her environment and a sense of socializing. This developmental process quickly snowballs into learning sophisticated forms of communication, which leads to a full-fledged personality. The entire process will not occur, however, unless parents respond to cries. It is this response that activates the intertwined process of intellectual, emotional, and personality development. Responding is to infants what the feel of cold water was to Helen Keller.

—Mark A. Hall

How to Use This Book

Hopefully, you have now developed a constructive attitude about crying. It isn't a medical condition, your child isn't suffering severely (only you are), and you won't spoil him. This book is meant to help you put that attitude into action.

The 79 ways are organized into different groups for convenient reference, based on the basic type of calming technique: oral solutions, physical needs, physical contact, motion, sound, and miscellaneous remedies. As you choose from these, keep in mind the following basic points.

IF IN DOUBT, FEED. If simply picking up and holding doesn't work, try feeding next. It is the single best pacifier, even if hunger is not the cause. If feeding doesn't work, then start to look through this list. You may want to come back to feeding if your child was too upset at first to eat.

MIX 'N' MATCH. A fundamental rule is that the more sensory modes (sound, motion, physical contact, etc.) you combine, the better. For example, one of our best combinations was to walk outdoors with our daughter in the snugli while singing and patting her back. Another sure bet with a strong multimedia dimension was to hold her in an outdoor Jacuzzi's warm, bubbling, illuminated water.

BE INVENTIVE. The key is experimentation and flexibility. Don't rigidly adhere to my ideas. Try your own. Some of the best solutions come at desperate times if you keep your mind open to different possibilities. For example, my husband and I came up with lots of new methods by applying the same principle in different situations. Once we learned that the sound of a running faucet was soothing, we thought to try the water sprinkler in the back yard, a fountain in the mall, and a waterfall in the woods.

DON'T EXPECT EVERY ONE TO WORK. These are methods that have worked for me or someone else at one point or another. Some may never work for your child. Others will work at one time but not another. It is sometimes said of calming techniques that everything works, but only for a while. That's why you need a wide variety to choose from. Read the introduction about the several phases of crying and ask yourself what makes sense for your child's particular age. A loud vacuum noise is magic for the newborn because it uses sound to drown out unpleasant sensations. It is miserable and frightening for the nine-month-old who is crying from boredom.

DON'T BE EMBARRASSED. Easier said than done, because a number of these will make you feel a little silly in public and will attract attention. Realize that this is less embarrassing and disruptive than the scene caused by a hysterical child. Rather than worrying that people are thinking you are a terrible parent, you can take pride in the thought that others will marvel at your inventiveness and persistence. Also, remember that if people stare, they are truly interested. It is only when they self-consciously look away that you have something to worry about.

DON'T GIVE UP TOO EASILY. Some techniques take a few minutes to catch on. Others only work at a milder level of upset. Therefore, you may have to persist for a while or come back to them after you have baby partially calmed down. An obvious example is a baby who is too upset to go to sleep. Similarly, parents can overlook the fact that a baby quite often will become too upset from hunger to eat.

DON'T GO OVERBOARD. It is necessary to emphasize the argument against spoiling because the spoiling myth is the greater danger. But it is possible to go too far the other way. Don't feel compelled to pick up your child at every whimper. You shouldn't feel that it is wrong to let her cry when other demands are more pressing, or that you should be expected to keep her quiet all the time. You can give your child too much of a good thing, and you will wear out the best tricks before you really need them.

DON'T BE STUBBORN. If it doesn't work after five minutes or so, try something else. Just because it worked yesterday doesn't mean it will today. There's no logic to some of these kids. If you have tried several methods from different categories, for a total of about twenty or thirty minutes, and none have worked, you should not exhaust yourself by mechanically going through the entire book. Select a technique or two that *you* like and try to stick it out. However, if it becomes unbearable, take a break, for however long you need, even if it means leaving the baby with someone else.

AVOID GUILT. If you can't control your child's crying, don't feel as if you have failed. It is not a mark on your parenting ability. I frequently was unable to calm my daughter, but at least I had the satisfaction that I tried my best and there was nothing else to do. Remember that babies cry as hard from minor disturbances as from real discomfort, so crying usually doesn't mean real suffering.

CONTROL YOUR ANGER AND FRUSTRATION. Sometimes you work yourself into a state of anger and frustration by trying too hard. You find yourself resenting your baby's behavior and so you try new methods with a vengeance. These feelings are a danger signal. They can lead to abusive behavior. Bouncing can become rattling. Patting can become pounding. This has happened to me and to other parents, so keep an eye out. It is a sign that you need a break. For both of your sakes, put the baby down until you regain your composure. Get your spouse to pinch hit (ouch).

ZEN AND THE ART OF BABY CALMING. Don't put your pride or parental self-image on the line. Adopt a try-and-see attitude, one where you almost don't care whether it works or not. I call this my "Zen" state, a sort of detachment from the process and a focusing of attention elsewhere. Turn on the TV for distraction. Compose poetry in your head. Recite your mantra. Pray for deliverance.

ORAL

SOLUTIONS

FEEDING

It is a fact that crying is often the result of hunger. It's equally true, but rarely mentioned, that babies also need to eat simply for comfort and security. For these reasons, one must forget all that propaganda about your angelic child enjoying nice, neat, scheduled feedings while lovingly wrapped in your arms. Believing this myth, like the one about Prince Charming, leads only to dangerous disillusionment. An infant's hunger and need for comfort are about as scheduled as the weather. Until solids are introduced, I urge you to adopt this brutally realistic approach: consider yourself a twenty-four-hour Dairy Queen. Always have a bottle at hand or wear shirts that lift up at a moment's notice.

Naturally, some fussy babies are difficult to feed. Here are some tips for feeding difficult eaters: Hold all meals in a quiet room, away from distractions. Some mothers go so far as to pull down shades to block stimulation. If you are coordinated and willing, some parents recommend feeding the baby while moving (standing, swaying, rocking all work well). Finally, it is imperative while feeding to restrain yourself from that extremely natural tendency to stroke, tickle, or comb any part of his body. As the author of *Spiritual Midwifery* aptly makes this point, it's like tickling someone as they make love – most intrusive.

THE MIGHTY BREAST

By all accounts, breast-feeding is somewhat better for babies. For fussy babies this is especially true. Breast milk is lower in fat so there is less concern about early obesity. Breast-feeding reduces the amount of air swallowed which often causes painful gas and crying. Nursing also relieves you of unnecessary worries that your baby's upset is caused by allergic reactions to his formula; your milk is a natural complement for your baby's body. Studies indicate many mothers needlessly worry that an inadequate milk supply is producing colicky behavior. If this is your concern, get junior weighed more frequently to remove this undermining self-doubt. Some nursing mothers find a direct correlation between foods they've eaten (nuts, chocolate, broccoli, for example) and increased fussiness in their baby. Be mindful of a possible connection between diet and crying. But, please, don't drive yourself crazy. For every mother who swears cow's milk is the culprit of their child's fretfulness, there is an expert debunking the theory that what Mamma eats affects her little one.

For Mom, nursing produces a hormone called prolactin, or the "perseverance" hormone, which naturally relaxes you. The more frequently—not intensely—junior sucks, the more prolactin there is soaking through your frayed body like deliciously warm water. When tension is running through your veins like poison and your baby is inconsolable, a time-out at the mighty breast is ideal. Don't ask yourself when the last feed was. It is not always about hunger—it's sometimes a matter of comfort and security.

To put your mind at rest, here are three things comfort sucking will *not* produce: a fat baby, a clingy baby, or a mother who never has her blouse buttoned. There are days when your child will need the extra tenderness that the breast provides. I recall one mother's horrified expression when she hissed that her three-week-old son "ate from nine until two in the morning yesterday." Some days your baby will eat practically all day and night. This is normal and, more important, it's the only way a child can increase your milk supply to meet his growing needs.

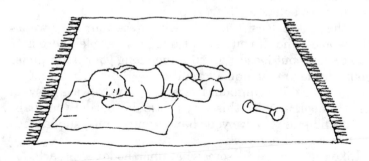

GIVE 'EM THE FINGER

This idea refers not to any physical expletive but rather to a pacifying trick for newborns that's literally right at your fingertips. Just put your pinkie onto the roof of baby's mouth, nail-side to tongue, and let her suck away. You may be shocked by the tornado force of her suck, a force strong enough to drink a McDonald's shake through a straw without any trouble. It may make you think that all her muscle coordination is between her gums.

This is a wonderful trick for those horrendous times when you're stuck with a crying baby and no real options. While driving I would often plug a pinkie into my daughter's mouth (she never took a *real* pacifier). Therefore, be prepared and make a habit of washing your hands as often as a dentist and keeping your pinkie nails trimmed to below the fingertip.

If the pinkie doesn't do the trick maybe your baby wants the whole hand. If you're built like most people, there is some tough but loose skin running along your palm under your pinkie and just above your wrist. Babies find it as succulent as filet mignon. However, it's not always easy for kids to hook up with this very particular part of your palm. So, it's helpful to move your hand around until she latches on like a snail to a rock.

Like the finger, this somewhat unorthodox approach

elicits stern stares from the uninitiated public, but don't worry. Do joggers worry about how they look when stretching their legs higher than their heads onto a tree trunk? Of course not. Nor should you worry when performing your parental fitness exercises.

THUMBS UP

Before having our baby, I self-righteously considered thumb-sucking a sure sign of mother-related insecurity. However, that unfounded opinion disappeared (along with so many others) instantly when realizing thumb-sucking's extremely useful application, namely, calming infants. What's best about the thumb is that it allows baby to calm *herself.* Sucking relaxes the stomach and other major muscles while also reducing eye movement. This response keeps outside stimulation and other world problems at bay. That is why you see thumb-suckers wearing an expression of casual indifference that seems to say, "Hey, I'm busy with this thumb. I'll catch the details, you know, later." Another advantage of thumbs is that, in contrast with pacifiers, the feeling of their own thumb being sucked teaches infants their first lessons about cause and effect.

However, keep in mind that excessive thumb-sucking may be a sign that your child is not having some other need met. Psychiatrists who studied thumb-sucking found that infants who sucked their thumbs tended to be fed on schedule, not demand. This could mean that the babies in the thumb-sucking group were left to fall asleep in a state of loneliness, without bottle-or-breast-toting parent on hand for comfort.

BAGELS & BONES

Bagels and bones are excellent tools for a quick oral fix, when it looks as though there's more teething than hunger going on. Bagels and bones are tasty but aren't consumed quickly. We used chicken leg bones scrubbed as clean as a skeleton in an anatomy class. Miniature or child-sized bagels are ideal, fitting perfectly into a baby's hand and mouth. Let's not get too fancy, though; it works equally well to cut a large bagel into several bits. In addition to bagels, French bread, hard buns, and melba toast all work well. Be careful, though, because there is always a chance of choking, as with any food more solid than applesauce. Carrots and hot dogs are particularly dangerous.

Another great solution for teething is to run an ice cube along the child's gums. Some parents may consider this too risky, but we often gave our daughter a big ice cube to play with until it melted into a precarious size.

33

THE MATERIAL WORLD

Even anti-Aprica parents can enjoy the rewards of this material world without compromising their values. I am speaking of cloth material, which, curiously, many babies like to suck. When acquiring your baby's material goods, the cheaper the better since l'enfant will be gumming it up. A blanket or towel or cloth diaper are best since all are generally sturdy enough—a mandatory feature—to hold up under heavy chomping stress. For teething, best of all are clean wet washcloths. A winning feature of this technique is that baby is virtually free of any choking threat while munching on, for example, a terry cloth towel.

THE RUBBER SURROGATE

Most babies are like catfish at the bottom of a fishbowl, forever sucking anything they can get their lips on, from blocks to socks. Pacifiers, which the British cleverly call "dummies," offer an easy way to satiate that indefatigable need to suck. It's a good idea to carry two pacifiers so that when one inevitably falls onto a vile sidewalk or subway floor, you are not left weaponless. Some smart parents string a cord through the pacifier ring and clasp it to a stroller or shirt so it never falls too far and is within reach for the child to reinsert. For safety reasons, *never* string a pacifier around your child's neck.

If your baby isn't taking to the pacifier, try different brands, styles, and sizes. Unfortunately, you may be like us and have landed a child who looks at a pacifier as if it were an unwelcome alien from another planet. If this is your problem, all I can offer is my most sincere condolences.

One final point for breast-feeders: it's probably best to wait until your baby is one month old before plugging a pacifier into that overactive mouth. Sucking on a pacifier may create what's called "nipple confusion." The way a baby sucks at the breast, the muscles she uses, are different from the method used with bottles or pacifiers. It takes more effort to suck from the breast. Wait until she's conquered breast sucking before introducing a surrogate.

PHYSICAL
NEEDS

I BEG YOUR PARDON

Getting a burp out of your baby expels air often swallowed while eating. This brings a type of supreme gratification only parents can appreciate. A sure sign that baby needs burping is if he is pulling on and off the bottle or breast. Babies sometimes need a burp *during* a meal, not only after. Each parent develops his or her own burping technique ranging from plain back pats to elaborate circles that move upward and end in a closing pat. All that really matters is that you are gentle. A harder pat doesn't produce more satisfying burps.

We should tell you, though, there are two sides to the burping story. Some naturalists consider burping a useless obsession of the Western world. Apparently, mothers in many primitive tribes have never heard of gas and their children survive quite nicely. "I often think if only burping failed to make a noise, there would be less concern about it," Dr. Hugh Jolly wryly concludes in his book on child care. So don't become too obsessed with passing the gas.

DIAPERS

It is one of the myths of parenting that babies cry because they need changing. Our observations are that a soiled diaper doesn't create enough discomfort to cause crying *until* a child has been baking in it for more than an hour. You can drive yourself nuts, waste a lot of money, and become an ecological hazard if you start changing the tot's diapers the minute whimpering starts. Although stewing in a soggy diaper seems absolutely unbearable to us big people, to babies a clean diaper is about as important as neatly stacked toys. Remember they just spent the last nine months in a warm, moist place. I am not encouraging you to leave your children in dirty disposables. Instead, I am suggesting that it is far from necessary to change diapers every time nature calls. This is especially true for newborns, who live solely on milk and therefore emit byproducts not nearly as noxious as do babies on solid foods.

DIAPER RASH

Mothers-to-be probably never envisioned the day when their gravest concern would be diaper rash and not Nicaraguan Contra aid or equal pay for equal work. But, alas, this will happen should your baby's bottom get raw and red as a fire engine. When diaper rash develops you can bet intense grizzly behavior does, too.

This multi-pronged plan of attack brings results and more quiet at home: soak baby in a bath doctored with about two tablespoons of baking soda, change diapers often, use plain soap and water instead of diaper wipes, and allow baby to spend time (nap time is ideal) naked from the waist down to give the painful problem an airing out. It is also helpful to use Desitin or a medicated ointment to protect baby's skin.

CLIPPING IT IN THE BUD

Little did you realize those sweet, perfect, tiny little toes and fingers on your baby carry the instruments of major destruction, specifically, self-destruction. Admittedly, there is something strange, almost unnatural about clipping a four-week-old's nails; it seems kind of like giving an infant a perm. But clip you must if you want to avoid pain-induced tears and red streaks lining your baby's body like Indian tribal paints. Babies grab their extremities with the force, discretion, and sense of wonder of a bargain shopper at a clearance sale.

Some children won't sit still long enough for you to complete a manicure or pedicure. For these squirming tots, try clipping nails while they sleep. Or, do as some parents suggest: bite their nails off. I've also found that using adult-style clippers works more effectively than those infant nail scissors that everyone seems to think are mandatory.

SLEEP

AHHHH, finally a solution you can embrace whole-heartedly. Sometimes a baby's crying is simply caused by fatigue. If you find yourselves thinking "enough is enough," chances are your child is, too. Why not do yourselves a favor by putting her to bed? I realize this is easier said than done, and there is not the space to go into all of the sleep-inducing techniques. Other books have been written on this specific problem. But I will give a few words of advice. Sometimes tired babies are too exhausted to sleep because their weariness has them too upset to drift off. You should be able to find an effective calming method in this book to get the baby quieted enough so that what is really needed– sleep–has a chance to take hold. A good calming session before putting baby to sleep acts as a soporific, kind of like drinking a mug of hot milk before bedtime.

There is virtually no reason to worry about her sleeping too long (just ask any experienced mother). And remember that some days she'll need three naps and others days a forty-five-minute nap will be enough. Take heart in one study showing that fussy babies are likely to sleep longer periods at night. Unfortunately, there are those occasional fussy babies who are fussy sleepers as well. This is an extraordinarily trying problem that has no simple solution.

A HEATED RESPONSE

Study after study claims keeping baby in a warm, almost hot, environment makes for a happier home. Researchers get pretty particular on this point, some suggesting eighty-eight to ninety degrees is best for stopping tears, while seventy-eight degrees is best for sleeping, others proclaiming the merits of a constant seventy-five degree environment. As you probably could guess at this point, it's suggested you try different temperatures to see what works.

When a baby is uncomfortably cold—and fussy babies are sensitive to this (it figures!)—she often cries just to raise her body temperature. It sure seems senseless to have your kid making life miserable when all you have to do is just to turn up the heat. Spring for a bigger utility bill this month for the sake of family happiness.

Other methods for staving off the sometimes cold shock of life include: putting baby to sleep stomach down in order to conserve heat; warming towels before giving her a bath; replacing diaper wipes with a washcloth dipped in warm water; warming sheets with a hot water bottle or electric heating pad, and using a lambskin (see "LAMBSKIN").

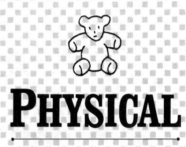

PHYSICAL
CONTACT

CARRYING ON

There is a sure test for detecting parents of fussy babies. They are the ones who can flawlessly make dinner, look up and dial phone numbers, dispense toothpaste, and do just about anything with one hand. This is because, next to feeding, holding your child is the single most effective form of pacifying. Babies need cuddling and companionship. Once your child can move, he will demonstrate how much he wants to be with you by following you around everywhere. Scientific studies of crying babies show that holding is the next best pacifier after feeding. One study found that babies carried for three extra hours a day cry forty-five percent less.

The trouble with wearing your baby all day is that this makes it almost impossible to get anything else done. Having a fussy baby gives one a new sense of appreciation for the handicapped. During the early months, you will find that one arm is incapacitated a great portion of the day. And even if you do find a convenient holding method, your picky child may insist on constant variety. So I set out several methods that have worked for me and others. But before I begin, let's once again address the question of spoiling.

For some reason the issue of spoiling is usually the most controversial when it concerns the act of picking up and carrying babies. Many of those parents who are against frequent holding are often the same ones who will overfeed crying babies. Rather than take a consistent stand against spoiling, they show a predisposition to assigning only physical needs (hunger) as the cause of all unhappiness and ignoring emotional and psychological needs. So the first answer to the spoiling argument is that one method of response is no more spoiling than another. You should simply do what works the best.

But, of course, two wrong responses don't make a right one, so the tough question is whether responding at all is proper. Of course it is. Particularly at the beginning, it is abusive and neglectful not to respond, and it goes against every instinct. Not responding teaches your child that the world is a cold and unresponsive place. (The Introduction includes a full discussion of the myth of spoiling.)

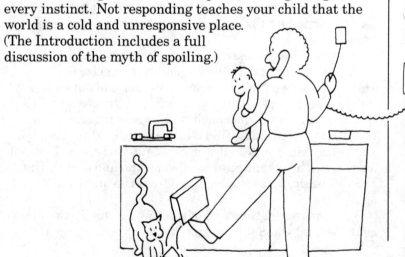

SLING

A simple contraption to carry your child close to you is a sling. The sling acts like a mini sitting hammock with the baby's fanny tucked into the material at your hip and her legs clipped around you. Your upper arm naturally acts as a backboard to keep her from flopping out. This position is excellent because it distributes the child's weight and gives you one arm and sometimes two hands free. Traveling with your baby in a sling is especially great when walking across fields or through crowded markets where strollers are as useless as a car.

Take a sturdy piece of material about four feet long, tie the ends into a secure knot, then place the material diagonally across your shoulder so that it drapes across the opposite hip (it's similar to the way scouts wear their merit badge sashes). If you are uncomfortable with the do-it-yourself approach, slings are often advertised in parenting magazines for under ten dollars. We found a nylon mesh type to be particularly strong and compact.

SNUGLI—NEVER LEAVE HOME WITHOUT IT

A snugli is a modern day papoose that goes in the front, sort of a knapsack with leg holes. ("Snugli" is the brand name of the leading model.) It swaddles baby next to your warm chest and directly over your soothing heartbeat, barricaded from that overstimulating world against the warm belly of another. The snugli is one of the most necessary pieces of baby paraphernalia. If you don't have one, get one. Plain and simple, a snugli can save your sanity during those trying first few months. You can see why babies love them; they are the closest thing in the cold cruel world to the womb. You can add to this near nirvana with a rhythmic back pat and a gentle sway in your walk.

The great advantage of the snugli is that you have both hands free, and the freedom of mobility. It's a perfect holding position. Mothers have had nine months practice at this position, so it feels easy and natural. However, the proximity of the milk supply may cause problems for some moms. Too many times when I did the carrying, our daughter would immediately begin rooting around like a puppy looking for its teat. Sometimes dads may have to carry the load.

Even after the baby passes the super fussy stage, the

snugli serves the invaluable purpose of a carry-along napping place. We wore ours while hiking and sightseeing all over Europe. No need to anticipate when to be back at the hotel for nap time because, like a tortoise with its home on its back, we had the crib on our stomach.

CLEAN SCHEMES

BATHING
Generally, a good long soak in the bath is a great quieter of mildly fussy babies, but not those who are in a full pitched wail. The operative word here for parents is *long*. Bathing is one solution that can work as long as you are willing to play lifeguard. Many parents find bathing along with baby to be mutually restorative. Tandem tubbing is a good way to relax together and strengthen the, no doubt, strained parent-baby bond. Be forewarned, though, that you'll probably reap more pleasure from dual bathing after the first two or three months, when your child grows somewhat sturdier than cooked spaghetti.

NOT BATHING
Some babies consider the whole process of bathing painful, threatening, flirting with death. The personal exposure of a bath is sometimes just too shocking to be fun, particularly for newborns. Parents of this baby should give themselves a break and forget total immersion bathing. Opt instead for sponge baths. Cleaning your baby, part by part, with a warm washcloth is just as hygienic.

Our mistake was considering it a parental duty to give our daughter a "real" bath—after all, they'd done it in the hospital. We felt shameful and insecure when we finally

stopped bathing her. One time her grandmother called and asked excitedly, "So, is she loving her baths the way all you kids did?" "Well, I wouldn't say she adores it yet," we replied, thinking of our tiny baby during her last bath screaming, trembling, gasping for breath and looking something like an electrocuted stalk of rhubarb. At about four months we resumed bathing and she did indeed adore it.

SHOWERS

Showering with baby offers a winning three-pronged approach to calming criers: it offers skin-to-skin contact, steamy, penetrating warmth, and the settling drone of white noise. What more could baby want? For the shower-master this task may prove to be frustrating if you expect to clean yourself in a traditional way. Holding anyone while showering makes washing yourself difficult and shampooing impossible. Both tasks are best forgotten to reduce frustration and risk.

JACUZZI

"La-de-da" you may say to this admittedly elite-sounding solution. But a Jacuzzi's warm, bubbly, brewing vat of illuminated water will unwind tension knotted up inside you and your crabby baby. For us, there was nothing more effective for relieving stress after dinner, after work, and after all the baby's good behavior had soured like milk left out in the ninety-degree sun. As far as baby goes, do not immerse her. Dangle her little feet in the water, making sure bubbles and rising steam are well within view. Leave baby *near* the heated water for *only* two-minute intervals for a total time of no more than ten minutes. It was under the spell of a Jacuzzi that our fussy daughter entered that nearly stupefied trance of total complacency we had seen and envied in our friends' children.

You don't have to romp with the BMW set to sleaze into a Jacuzzi. Be bold, be brave, and look like you belong when you sneak into a nearby apartment complex equipped with a Jacuzzi. Just make sure it isn't singles or couples only.

THE RUB DOWN

TUMMY RUBS

Some experts believe massaging your colicky baby's abdomen can help relieve pain. Even if this method fails to produce stunning effects, at least you can be consoled knowing you've given your child one of nature's truest expressions of love. Here are specifics for an effective massage. Laying baby on her back, use your fingers—tips flattened—to knead her softly with both hands from just below the ribs to just above the hip joint on your right, her left. Stroke repeatedly, softly and steadily. Then, using the same technique, move across her abdomen from your left to right. Repeat several times. Next, you combine those two motions into one big motion and repeat. Finally, massage the area from just above her hip to below her ribs and repeat. Next, combine all three motions into one sweeping movement and repeat.

Don't press and poke your baby as if she were built like Jim McMahon of the Chicago Bears. Treat her like a delicate piece of china. Keep her warm, touch gently, move slowly and steadily, and always rub clockwise along the abdomen. It's best to begin with a short massage, then build from there. As odd as it sounds, infants need to get used to massage. This technique can actually move baby's gas through the colon, so don't be surprised if you hear sound effects. Some parents say it's best to give an abdominal massage in a bath when baby is less likely to be tense. If baby isn't relaxed to begin with, this plan will probably be a failure. In this case, give in...but don't give up—try again later.

BACK RUBS

Chances are you deserve a back rub every bit as much as your child does. Perhaps more. But I'll leave it up to mom and dad to decide who needs babying more. Back rubs fall into the category of preventive medicine. A few soft and steady strokes along your baby's back can postpone a crying episode. It's best, if you can, to lay him stomach down so pressure is exerted against his tummy. If your kid

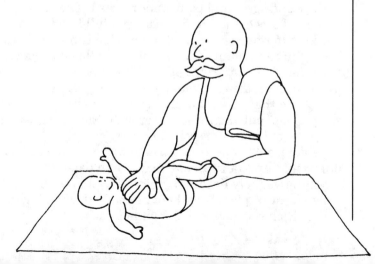

won't go for that, just sit him in your lap and perform a vertical back rub.

Colicky babies tend to tense their bodies, making it hard to massage them. These suggestions may help: place baby's body on a half-filled warm water bottle, or drape him over a beach ball (more on that under "KINKY RELIEF").

BACK PATTING

There's nothing like a good pat on the back to make you feel better, and the same holds true for the fussy baby. This method is particularly good for the skin-sensitive or uncuddly baby. Once baby is in a relatively settled mood, lay her down in bed or on a couch, pull up a comfortable chair, and begin very gently but firmly patting her back with your fingers and palm outstretched. The bouncy surface of a bed and the firmness of a full-handed pat combine to reverberate soothing motion throughout the body. You can enhance this motion by following the pat with a slight left-to-right jiggle. Experiment by varying the mix of speed, strength, and jiggle to produce just the right effect, one that seems to send hypnotic messages of "sleep, sleep, sleep" pulsing through her body. Slow, firm pats at a rate of about one per second are best.

It's advisable to prohibit anyone with that queer but prevalent (especially among men) compulsion to drum on anything vaguely flat from performing this trick. Any baby—fussy or placid—will not be soothed when having a Buddy Rich solo pounded out on her back.

KINKY RELIEF

Despite what you might be thinking, this is a smorgasbord of solutions aimed at relieving kinks that can grip a baby's intestinal system like rubber bands wrapped around a golf ball. Folding baby over a beach ball helps relieve stomach pains. This method demands careful parental supervision to guard against flopping off.

A less demanding plan involves simply rolling up a cloth diaper and inserting it under the belly of your baby when she's lying down. This technique offers strategic padding for those more masochistic colicky kids who thrust their knees up into their stomachs. A hot water bottle also works well, but make sure the water isn't too hot, just comfortably warm.

A dependable standby form of Kinky Relief is jiggling baby across your knees. Place baby, stomach down, along your lap, and move your legs nervously like you're in a dentist's waiting room about to have a root canal. Finally, some veteran moms claim giving baby some warm water ten minutes prior to feeding time helps iron out abdominal kinks. One mother I know swears a tiny dose of Ginger Ale does the trick.

WORKING IT OUT

No sweatbands, striped leotards, or disco beat is needed for this exercise plan. It reduces crying, not body size. Try sitting baby up, somehow supporting her so she won't flop over, and move her arms up and down as if she were doing a 1960s-style dance like the swim. Laying her on her back, try the same thing using her legs instead. These simple calisthenics are harmless, provided you keep away from any rigorous, Fonda-esque routines. Admittedly, some hysterical babies will not take too kindly to this, but sometimes the pure astonishment of a new sensation will do the trick.

LAMBSKIN

Putting a lambskin in the crib may seem as ostentatious as outfitting your baby in mink baby booties. However, a patch of cuddly lambskin can go a long way toward getting your baby to sleep and keeping him that way! Landing on this fur is never startling like a cold sheet can be, so, when it comes time to deposit baby into the crib your risk of waking him, and of your (if you're normal) exploding in a fit of frustration, are greatly reduced.

Lining a carseat or stroller with lambskin provides a soft surface that invites sleep and guarantees a comfortable ride cushioned from jarring bumps and turns. Lambskin is terrific for overnight traveling as well. The blissful continuity of sleeping on the same patch of fur reduces disruption and the resulting anxiety and wakefulness traveling can cause.

Despite its somewhat fancy and frivolous appearance, lambskin is washable (use a delicate cycle). And, lambskin is just as effective in hot weather because it absorbs sweat and allows some air to circulate. You can find lambskins for about $40 at leather shops, some baby stores, and in advertisements in the back of parent/baby magazines.

SWADDLING

Since time immemorial swaddling has stopped many an infant from crying. Studies conducted recently proclaim swaddling to be "the most effective" quieter of small babies (newborn to six weeks old). Even the baby Jesus is shown tightly swaddled in his baby pictures, though one doubts somehow that he was a colicky child.

Wrapping baby snuggly into a receiving blanket (or any small piece of cozy cloth) comforts him, but more important, it inhibits his "Moro reflex," the involuntary movement that often startles a baby and makes him cry. This restraint is especially important for colicky children who often are less able to buffer disturbances brought on by their own bodies.

The best swaddling material is light and slightly stretchy (this helps achieve a tighter tuck). A flannel sheet is good in summer. British child expert, Penelope Leach, suggests swaddling a baby with his arms bent at the elbow, legs flexed, and hands free in case he wants to suck. It is perfectly safe to swaddle a baby before putting him to bed. In fact, it is a good idea.

WEDGING

This is yet another method for buffering your baby from the big, bad world. Often it is those sudden spastic movements which we all have gone through when drifting off to sleep that startle a newborn, waking him, and usually generating another bout of crying.

Here's how to do it: Lay baby on his right side with his back pressed against the crib bumpers, head touching the front of the crib. Then, place a rolled-up towel or pillow against his abdomen. This provides some pressure but mainly keeps him tucked in place. Some crafty parents transform an opened dresser drawer or a cardboard box with the top cut off into a custom-sized, pre-wedged crib.

MOTION

MOTION

Although newborn babies arrive somewhat physically incapacitated and mentally incoherent, they have well-developed senses. Their sense of motion is particularly developed. After all, your baby has lived through many months of jostling in the womb, and, no doubt, you have experienced some of her movements yourself. If you think about it, motion, not stillness, is the natural state for a newborn who has been in almost continuous motion since conception.

There are a couple of general thoughts to keep in mind as you read through these specific techniques. First, there is no one magic speed or type of motion. Some babies respond best to gentleness, others like surprising amounts of force, and most like some of each at different times: gentle to maintain calm, forceful to overcome a fit. The key is *consistency*. Think in terms of mesmerizing, like a hypnotist, rather than jarring like a carnival ride. Second, our vestibular system, the apparatus in our inner ears that senses motion, is structured to detect motion in three directions: up and down, back and forth, and side to side. Therefore, when the opportunity presents itself, it is usually true that the best distraction comes from movement in all three directions (not all at once, of course, but in a repetitive sort of routine).

ROCK ON WITH YO' BAD SELF

If you hold the stereotyped image of the placid infant who is rocked peacefully to sleep each night, you may find, as I did, that the rocking chair is a frustrating disappointment. Its subtle motion makes it too subdued for the difficult kid. Don't abandon this old standard too quickly, though. The rocking chair still may be excellent preventive medicine. When your baby seems on the verge of a breakdown, taking to the rocker can head off an outburst. However, it usually only worsens the full-pitched wail.

The best way to rock is at a rate of about one per second, moving about three inches back and forth from the center. Theory has it that this simulates the natural movement that is felt in the womb when walking at a normal pregnant pace. If you're like me and have knobby shoulders, it may help to drape something soft over your shoulder to provide a cushioned resting place. Besides holding baby against your chest, another favorite position is to sit baby on your lap and wrap your arm across her stomach like a seat belt (the pressure against baby's stomach can ease pain). And, unless it is too cold, never rule out rocking outside at night. Fresh air and gentle evening sounds are marvelous prevention for those particularly intense fussies that set in when the sun goes down.

FRONTAL ROCK

No, this isn't a new strain in New Wave music. It is an innovative rocking position for a pint-sized baby who likes a little scenery with his ride. Lay baby face down on your legs with his head looking out beyond your knees. If your chair has a foot rung, prop your heels on it like a cowboy sitting on a bar stool, except keep your knees and thighs together. This should allow a snug position from which baby can look out as you rock. You can also pat his back at the same time. This position is more comfortable for you than the standard since it takes no effort to hold him. If you have a steady hand, it's possible to read something light – meaning paperbacks or magazines. Holding up a hard-bound version of *War and Peace* gets pretty hard after the first five minutes.

THE CRADLE OF JOY

A cradle is another classic mothering tool, one you might expect to find only in the Waltons' bedroom or in a Whistler painting, hardly one suited for the modern-day infant born with the help of coaches, Lamaze and probably some stiff drugs. But, like many of the classics, a cradle remains extremely effective today. It offers that rare and blissful opportunity of rocking your baby *without* holding her.

The beauty of the cradle lies in its simplicity: there are no moving parts, or rather, it is one big moving part, sort of like the womb itself. But I don't mean to excessively venerate the traditional. If this book has any message, surely it is that you should not hesitate to try improving on tradition. For example, the truly decadent do their rocking while lying in bed with the cradle at arm's length. Or better yet, try this idea passed along by some inventive parents: tie a rope securely to the end of a cradle so you can pull it and thus start the cradle rocking in the middle of the night, instantly upon hearing the slightest yelp, yawn, or predawn moan.

BABY MOSES

Moses was saved by a reed basket; it can do the same for you and your baby. Lay him in a four-foot-by-one-foot reed basket that is cushioned with soft blankets, grab the handles tightly together in one hand, and swing smoothly front and back, like a pendulum.

The flexible sides of the basket wrap around him snugly and the gentle swing lulls most babies right to sleep. If this doesn't work at first, try swinging faster and harder. You'll be surprised at how much he likes centrifugal force. (Maybe he's a budding astronaut.) Like the thrill of a roller-coaster ride, the force seems to overwhelm the other senses, including whatever is causing him to cry.

One bonus of the Baby Moses approach is that your baby is already tucked into a cozy bed so that, if he drifts off to sleep, he's already in bed. You can pick up these all-purpose reed baskets pretty cheaply at those import stores that carry lots of straw things, or at little concession stands along the Nile. Make sure the basket is very sturdy before swinging your precious progeny to and fro.

71

PORCH SWING

A porch swing is another wonderful way to relax with baby. It combines a soothing swinging motion with nature's best tranquilizer—fresh air. This worked best when we held our daughter in our lap so she looked out at the vast world before her. Porch swings are also an extremely effective tool for lulling babies to sleep. In addition, they make an excellent platform for that all-too-rare event, namely, an *uninterrupted* conversation with a spouse, friend, or colleague.

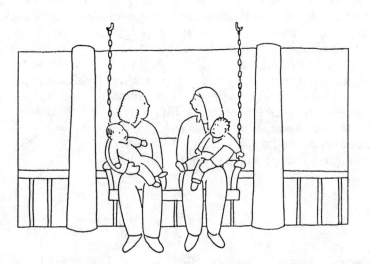

MATTRESS MAGIC

If I had to pick our one best technique, this would probably be it. It has been our most enduring salvation from insanity and incapacitating frustration.

Hold baby against your chest with one arm (let's say the right) under her buttocks so that her head rests on your shoulder. Use your other (left) arm to pat her back or cup her head. Stand on a mattress and slowly bounce while shifting your weight from left to right. Practice your technique by bouncing gently two or three times on one side before shifting weight to the other leg. Do this as long as you can stand it (which is usually to the point where the room begins to look like a television screen with a loose vertical hold knob).

You can augment your technique with all sorts of extras. What worked well for us was humming a monotone note softly into her ear or patting her back gently, or both. Wrapping a soft blanket across baby's back is also helpful when sleep is the goal (and when is it *not* the goal?). The really expert bouncer can put a twist into the back and forth movement that results in something like a figure eight pattern. This produces the optimal stimulation because it results in movement in all three dimensions (up and down, back and forth, and front and back.) After a while, it all begins to look like a one-man band. If you can pat your head and rub your stomach at the same time, you'll be great at this.

Be careful doing this one in the middle of the night when you are half asleep, especially if you have poor balance. It's easier than you think to fall off the bed.

One final note: show baby-sitters this trick and laugh a lot while explaining this truly magical remedy to the politely incredulous adolescent. She may laugh at you then, but she'll thank you later.

THE MATTRESS JIGGLE

This is a good down-and-dirty method when you need your hands free for a couple of minutes to put on makeup or tie a half Windsor. Just plop your child down onto the bed and jiggle the mattress with your foot placed close to him. Generally, a faster jiggle is good for stopping a cry while a slower one maintains calm. An alternative for less delicate tasks, such as concentrating on a phone call, is simply to sit on the bed and bounce.

THE BABY AND THE TRAMP

For those with a gymnastic bent, a trampoline is a Jim Dandy pacifier. You can use either the backyard variety or spring for a minitramp to keep around the house. If friends ask why you have one in the bedroom, you can always explain that you and your spouse are working your way through the Kama Sutra. That may be easier to understand than admitting that you are trying to calm your baby by imitating a mamma kangaroo.

With the full-sized model, there is the need to exercise extreme restraint. The temptation to try out those leg tucks learned in elementary school can be burning. For that reason, we suggest you bring along another adult so you can get a solo workout on the trampoline.

BABY BOUNCINETTE

These are like bouncing lounge chairs for babies. The
"bouncinette" is designed to let your baby bounce gently
while she plays, sits, or sleeps. The slightest movement
from your baby generates a stream of bouncing that, as the
ad proclaims, "brings gurgles of delight." If all that is true,
it may well be worth the $35 since you not only get a happy
baby, you get to put the kid down by herself for awhile. The
New Yorker magazine generally carries an ad for this
product of the baby boomlette era.

BABY SWING

The person who invented the free-standing baby swing
deserves a Nobel Peace Prize. With its wind-up crank that
keeps baby swinging for fifteen or twenty heavenly
minutes without any effort. The steady motion seems to
lull most high-maintenance babies into a rare state of
contentment.

Most models require your baby to sit up in a chair, which
makes it necessary to wait until she gains some physical
control over her limbs before using the baby swing. When
that happens, I recommend propping her up and securing

her in with folded blankets, placed strategically. A better alternative is the deluxe model that has a detachable bassinet. This allows use of the swing for the youngest newborns and for bedtime rocks.

As the magic of most calming methods eventually wears out, it is best to use this lifesaving method only when you are in real need of two hands. Mealtimes seem to be a favorite for employing the baby swing.

JOLLY JUMPER

This solution is a derivative of the jungle gym, only made for those under twenty-five inches tall. A Jolly Jumper (one of the popular brands) is a swell piece of apparatus that is part swing, part trampoline, and totally wonderful for exercising the blues right out of your cranky kid. Basically, it's a cloth seat that is attached to metal springs that hang from a metal chain which is attached to a door frame. They look like unwieldy contraptions at first, but don't worry, they always come with instructions that are usually illustrated, thank God.

Jolly Jumper is quite simply fascinating to babies, once they've gotten over the inevitable phase of fear about what Mommy is doing to me now. First of all, the contraption allows baby to stand up which, in itself, is novel. Secondly, the springy coil enables him to bounce to his heart's content each time his foot hits the floor. (You may be surprised how quickly your kid catches on to this causal relationship.) In this way, the Jolly Jumper is like the baby bouncinette (see "BABY BOUNCINETTE") because the child's own movement stimulates more movements, thereby making the helpful hand of a parent delightfully unnecessary.

Before our daughter could crawl but seemed itchy to get moving, the Jolly Jumper was the perfect satisfier. Sick as this sounds, we used to say "it's time to string her up," meaning to the J.J. of course, so we could get through a meal without interruption. Everyone would be humored, including us, as we looked at our daughter happily bouncing away like a marionette dressed in a girdle.

THE SUPER BABY-HOLD

No cape is needed for this trick, only a pair of steady hands. Press your palms flat against baby's stomach, tuck your fingers around his sides, lift him above your face (a beaming parental smile is suggested), and slowly move this bundle back and forth. The pressure of your palms against his stomach can offer nice relief from the abdominal pain often associated with colicky or fussy babies. Engine sound effects help achieve the total flying sensation. Note: some babies will not like all this space around them, so use your discretion.

WOMB WALKING

As appalling as it may sound at this point, imagine you are pregnant. This remedy requires you to simulate the position your baby was inside the womb (remember, she was right side up just before she rolled over to come out). Press baby tightly against your stomach, head toward the left side of your chest so she'll be in the best position for listening to the reassuring sounds of your heartbeat. Then wrap your arms along the side of her body, your hands locking like a swing seat around her behind, and begin walking at a relaxed pace. This position is a bit awkward, but it provides a cozy and familiar nest in which baby can curl up and, hopefully, fall asleep. (It also gives dad a great opportunity to learn what it was like for nine months.)

Putting baby down to sleep from this position is a bit tricky. But most parents quickly become very adept at the fine art of contortion, finding just the right combination of lean, tuck, twist, and toss to land her in bed without disturbance. Womb walking is best for those early weeks when the baby is still light and less of a strain on your back.

SOME PLIÉS, PLEASE

A little ballet know-how is all that's needed for this gem. Carrying your baby in the over-the-shoulder hold, place your heels together, toes pointing out, and bend at the knees (without lifting your heels); then, pull your thighs together to straighten back up. This is called first position. Second position is the same except your feet are spread about two or three feet apart. You may find second position easier if your sense of balance isn't that great.

This method is great for carving away those postnatal pudgies wrapped around the calves, thighs, and buttocks. However, to maximize its exercise potential, the plié must be done fairly slowly. A count of four is suggested. A less graceful alternative, but one that is just as effective, is to do the same thing much faster, to a count of one. I call this the "Oom-pah Dance." Humming or some rhythmic background music you can sing along with is good accompaniment. Repeat as long as your body holds up and your baby keeps quiet.

HAMMOCK HOLD

This is a technique for those who like the outdoors or who have an extraordinarily large living room. Lying down on a hammock, tightly hold your baby against your chest and swing gently back and forth. Perhaps a little serenade will help him forget the fussies faster. Perhaps a little Pina Colada will help you do the same. What's extra special about the hammock hold is that you get to lie down on the job! Don't be tempted to leave him in the hammock by himself, no matter how deep it is and how immobile baby seems. It only takes one time for an accident to occur.

SWIVEL CHAIR

Just hold baby either in your lap or over your shoulder, dig your feet into the floor, and twist left and right. The pace depends on baby first, your stomach second. Often it helps to begin at a faster clip to offset an impending cry. However, as with the rocker, swiveling is more effective at prolonging quiet times than calming a crying baby. A swivel session can be accompanied by songs or a good television show to offset parental boredom.

SWAYING

The real trick here is in the softness of your sway. Take one of those deep breaths you learned in birthing class and think of standing on a sunny beach in Hawaii and swaying with the gentle ocean breeze. Begin your left-to-right sways with a soft curl of the shoulder that ripples into a subtle twist at the waist. A good way to put more sashay into your sway is to bend the knee on the side you are turning toward and slightly pivot on the balls of your feet. Reggae music lends itself quite nicely to a swaying session, but use your musical imagination to suit your own tastes.

BABY STEPS

Even men who refuse to dance with their wives end up dancing with their fussy babies at some desperate moment. Dancing is a very pleasant and effective way of entertaining your child. Here's where it comes in handy to be versed in ballroom technique, especially the waltz and rumba. If you're not, don't worry—any gliding motion with some sort of beat will suffice nicely. You can dance cheek-to-cheek, but it's often more enjoyable for baby if you prop her on your arm and hold her out a bit for some eye-to-eye contact. Babies like to focus on their parents.

As you create your unique baby dance, try to move in as many directions as possible (up and down, front and back, and side to side). This provides maximum stimulation to baby's highly developed motion sensory system. You don't necessarily need music, but it adds to the effect. The chapter on sound gives lots of advice, but for quick reference I will mention that our child and others I know seem to have a special fondness for off-beat genres such as reggae and bluegrass but don't go in for the currently popular punk and heavy metal. Babies must be born with more aesthetic sensibility than we first suspect, but somewhere along the line most seem to lose it.

MACHINE DREAMS

WASHING MACHINE

Using a washing machine to do your dirty work is great
when a hands-on approach to curing the fussies is
impossible. Strap baby into a car seat or infant seat, secure
the seat safely on top of the washer, hold on tight, and
start' er up. The combination of vibration and sound
envelop a baby as effectively as any recommended solution.
For those fussy babies who need a whole lotta shakin' goin'
on to quiet down, just advance the machine to its spin cycle

and let 'er rip. We used this technique to gobble a quick dinner together without having to pass a screaming tot back and forth.

Needless to say, it's more economical if you throw in a load of wash while sending baby on a pleasure ride. In the unlikely event you don't have any dirty laundry, turn on the machine anyway! The half-hour of quiet is surely worth a few wasted watts of electricity.

THE DRIER

The same idea as the washer, only with some added benefits. For one thing, there is all that moist heat which turns a lounge on the drier into a luxurious sauna. Fussy kids love warmth. Being perched atop a drier also offers a nice consistent ride for kids who find the shifting gears of a washer a bit too disruptive and enjoy a constant purring sound vibrating through their little limbs. For parents, driers are a nice option since you can set the timer to whatever duration is called for. Again, make certain baby is securely fastened on top of the drier. It is crucial that you never leave the baby unattended during any appliance ride.

THE DISHWASHER

Same principles and instructions as the washer and drier. One strong plus with the dishwasher is that its kitchen location allows you to accomplish something like making dinner while supervising your child's ride. Often the washer-drier are tucked away and thereby made less convenient to the parent in search of a calmer baby. Not to restate the obvious, but I'm talking about placing your baby on top of the dishwasher—not in it.

FRONT-LOADING WASHERS
The makers of this dying breed of washer gave a gift to fussy babies and their suffering families. How absolutely perfect that the window to a world of whirling, churning, gurgling wash is at the baby's eye level. In most cases, your fussy child will remain completely involved in this trick for the duration of the wash. Just place him in his car seat directly across from the washer window and relax.

Many laundromats still use front-loaders, so this option is around. If you're desperate and have some wash to do, I urge you to go and make a spectacle of yourselves. For this outing, though, it's probably a good idea for you to leave the car seat in the car and park your kid in front of the machine in a stroller. After all, customers will need to get through the aisles, and that should make it easier.

GETTING CARRIED AWAY

Remember those old-time carriages with big white rubber wheels the size of frisbees and super bouncy springs? Admittedly they were a bit bulky and ill-suited to the plastic collapsibility that typifies this day and age of trunk-sized baby products. But they worked magic for fussy babies. All you had to do was jiggle and swiggle and tap the handle bar and baby's fussiness dissolved into a sea of soothing movements. Only the most miserable unhappy child could keep crying in the midst of such tranquillity.

We rediscovered the Grand Old Carriage during a visit to England, where the suspicion of "progress for progress' sake" mentality has preserved many fine traditions. There, we saw mothers sitting through entire church services—without one trip outdoors—while bouncing their babies in carriages. The beauty of the pram is its ability to perform without walking an inch, which is perfect for parents unavoidably caught in the stationary mode. Another bonus is its cavernous space for putting groceries or library books or even a second child placed neatly in the front end.

Unfortunately for us on the frontier side of the Atlantic, these old-style carriages are hard to come by. They have largely disappeared except for antique stores, attics, and designer baby boutiques.

KEEP ON STROLLING

There's nothing like a little fresh air and a change of scene to quiet a screaming baby. For parents, even a quick stroll around the block can be as relaxing as an hour-long massage. Even if it's cold or raining, you can just pack your stroller into the trunk of the car and head to the nearest mall or supermarket, or, if you're lucky, good museum.

A harmful side effect that can develop from strolling is unnecessary spending. All you did was set out on a spontaneous excursion to escape the cacophony of screams bouncing off of all four walls and somehow, you find your-self coming home with frivolous appliances, bric-a-brac, and extra supplies of things you never use to begin with.

This is not a simple coincidence. Shopping sprees have long been recognized as a universal salve for all sorts of emotional injury. For first-time moms, this can send your self-esteem plummeting as you grapple with the stereotype of your new domestic identity. The simple remedy: leave your money at home.

Be forewarned that some infants HATE strolling. No matter how fine the weather or how many toys dangle from the safety bar, you will confront only disaster as you promenade down the street with your unstrollable child. If yours, like ours, is one of those rare infants afflicted with

this unfortunate condition, take heart; it won't be too many months before she will be pulling you out the door for a stroll, like a master being walked by his dog.

ELEVATOR

An elevator ride is a simple way to lift your baby out of his fussy mood. The motion is quite subtle compared with other methods, but the gut-gripping pull of gravitational force is such a novel sensation that it distracts most babies from their woes. If you have access to a high rise, the big

ride that goes directly to the top floors is preferable.

What do you do as you shuttle up and down aimlessly? I recommend bringing along a walkman, a friend, or an idea that needs mulling over. If you run into the same people, explain that you are studying the social psychology of elevator conversation for your master's thesis or that your child was born with an inexplicable addiction to Muzak.

MOTOR TRENDS

Cruising the streets and highways is considered one of the most sure-fire ways of calming a fussy baby. Some parents swear that driving with their baby works one-hundred percent of the time. And, a strong feature of this method is that it requires very little physical effort. If you are caught in stop-and-go driving, or waiting at a red light, quickly begin jiggling the car seat with your free hand to simulate that soothing driving motion.

Be forewarned, though, that this doesn't work equally well for every fusser. Some babies are silenced after only a mile or two. Then, there are those kids who need to travel across a few county lines before heading into dreamland. And, then, there are babies like ours who begin wailing simply at the sight of car keys.

BABY EXPRESS

In urban areas, mass transit is an excellent calming method that has the added bonus of getting you out of the house. The constant motion, the hypnotic vibration buzzing under your skin, and variety of sounds emitted by trains, buses, subways and planes are soothing to most babies. One mother I know rode a New York City bus each morning beginning at five to keep her fussy baby from crying. The mom was tired, but not nearly as frayed as she would have been had she remained cooped up inside with her crying baby.

Mass transit also offers a variety of other calming distractions. You can look out windows at passing scenery, peer over the seat back at the person behind you, or play with those dangling grips used by standing passengers. But sometimes the easiest silencer is simply to lay your baby down on his stomach next to you on the seat or in a safe carrier. This provides maximum absorption of motion and a place to lie when he falls asleep.

The best attitude to adopt is to treat your public vehicle as a home away from home. Walk around, sing, read baby books—whatever it takes. That grumpy-looking man staring at you from across the aisle will brighten up with a few charming baby smiles. We used to make a game out of breaking through the stony anonymity of mass-transit commuters. Remember to wear a discreet outfit for breast-feeding in case a snack is needed. And never avoid nursing a hungry baby because you are in public. A quiet baby is of much greater interest to fellow passengers than how you manage the mechanics of discreet breast-feeding.

SLEEPTIGHT

If your baby calms down the moment your car tires hit the pavement, you might consider SleepTight, a new product that simulates the sound and motion of a car traveling 55 m.p.h. This elaborate machine was invented by a man who was nearly overwhelmed by his colicky son five years ago. According to the extensive testing and research that led to FDA approval of SleepTight, it quiets eighty-five percent of colicky babies within four minutes. Surely, this beats those two-in-the morning drives down deserted streets.

The machine itself consists of two well-crafted pieces. One is a small box which produces white noise, the same sound that wind makes blowing past a car window on the interstate. The other part is a three-and-a-half pound motor unit that vibrates the crib as if it, too, were moving along the highway at the speed limit. Installation is a bit tricky, but a bigger obstacle may be the price. SleepTight is a big-ticket item, costing $69.95 plus shipping. (Call 1-800-325-3550 to order.) This noninvasive solution to severe colic may be worth it, though.

SOUND

SINGING

So what if you're not the next Whitney Houston, just belt out a few tunes for your baby anyway. You'll soon discover babies are delightfully indiscriminate audiences. (Under the mystified gaze of a four-month-old, a few too many parents develop grandiose ideas about their musical talents.) Sing anything—Buddy Holly, Frito-Lay commercials, hymns, your alma mater, as well as traditional favorites like Old McDonald and Pat-A-Cake. One couple we know swears by the theme song from "Mister Ed." Another friend claims foreign national anthems are the most effective silencers. As odd as it seems, babies are born with musical tastes and may, like our child, prefer Pure Prairie League to the Pretenders. Stay in tune with your baby's favorites and repeat those hits as often as necessary.

99

HUMMING

If you think humming to yourself is reserved for those on the nerdish side of happy, think again. Most fussy babies adore vibrating, wordless serenades. Don't hum softly out of self-consciousness, as you might when riding an elevator. For this fairly simple method to work, you must hum from the diaphragm and project. It's best to begin with a strong and continuous hum the moment you detect your child is heading for a good cry. The first note hummed is like a traffic light turning red...it stops baby in his whinny tracts. Humming increases your repertoire immensely, since no words are needed to get through a song.

MUSIC BOXES

A few dollars spent on a music box is a wise investment indeed. A music box, preferably a size a child can manipulate with his hands and mouth, will silence moderate fussing fits. In our house we must have heard "White Christmas" five hundred times, and this was in Arizona in ninety-degree springtime! It got to the point where we'd sing our own lyrics that began: "I'm dreaming of a perfect baby...just like the one I thought I'd have..." A key feature of music boxes is their compact portability. Bring one wherever you go, especially if you're shy about singing in public.

MUSICAL MOBILES

This suspended merry-go-round of animals, clowns, or balloons can fascinate even the most tear-bound baby. Just wind up the tune and let kiddy classics like "You Are My Sunshine" or "Twinkle Twinkle" serenade your baby. Make sure you put baby within viewing distance of the mobile. Infants enjoy watching the slow-turning circles of a mobile just as much as listening to the simple songs.

Don't let your baby's size prevent you from employing one of the most popular (and useful) shower gifts around. If your baby can't sit up on his own you can either hold him at eye-level to the mobile, or, better yet, plunk a car seat into the crib and place him safely inside it.

SOME MOTHER GOOSE, MAESTRO

A little "Hey diddle, diddle" can go a long way toward quieting a fussy baby at dinner time, or anytime for that matter. Invest in a Mother Goose record or nursery rhyme tape. Yes, this is a command. Usually children's libraries carry these records, so check one or two out and find a way to tape them. Tapes are preferable to records since you'll (hopefully) find that music works wonders in the car as well. There is something mysteriously all-engrossing about children's music, even to a tiny four-month-old. One negative side effect for the parent is that you'll inevitably get "Bah, bah, black sheep" or some such tune stuck in your mind like a hideous commercial jingle. Nonetheless, this trick is worth that potential annoyance.

REGGAE

The melodic, mellow, and at times monotonous beat of the island music called reggae acts as a musical tranquilizer for fussy babies. One night I happened to turn on a Caribbean music show. I noticed our baby growing more still, kind of jiving to that heavy four-four bass beat. Pretty soon, we were both swaying softly to the sounds of Toots and the Maytalls, Rita Marley, and Jimmy Cliff, and breathing a little deeper, too. The next day I checked out some reggae tapes at the public library, including Bob Marley's Christmas carols. Quite simply, this music is magic.

Following the initial delight at discovering a new, easy method for quieting our baby, panic set in thinking I was breeding a marijuana-worshiping Rastafarian. I envisioned her smoking cigar-sized joints, refusing to comb her hair, and asking Santa for money to attend the annual springtime reggae festival in Jamaica. I wanted a calm baby, but not that badly.

TAPE SENSATIONS

If you're one who sneers at numerology, gags on tofu, and is suspicious of anything with the word "cooperative" in its title, please try to open your mind to this suggestion. Even children of arch conservatives are calmed by tapes of gently flowing waterfalls blended with whispering violins and a moaning harp or two. So-called "New Age" tapes really can quiet a crying child—no personal mantra, guru, or aura analysis needed. This music kind of melts into the air like incense and before you know it, you too may be mellowing somewhat. As spiritual leaders would advise, don't resist— you could probably stand some non-narcotic unwinding yourself.

WOMB HITS OF THE '80S

Even stodgy child experts recommend playing a tape of womb noises to quiet a crying baby. This suggestion is not as way-out as it seems when you consider that so many other methods—snuggling, swaddling, rocking, and jiggling —are aimed at simulating the womb environment. Why not just invest about six bucks for the real McCoy if it works? Those swooshing, thumping, gurgling noises may strike you as appealing as a dripping faucet. But, hey, this is just a sneak preview of the all but inevitable battle ahead of conflicting musical tastes between parent and child.

If you're thinking this is all rubbish, consider the findings of a Japanese obstetrician who recorded the womb noise of several pregnant women. When Dr. Hajime Murooka played back these noises for crying newborns, 83.9 percent of them calmed down and one-third were asleep within minutes. Often these taped womb noises are marketed in the form of a stuffed animal or inside a pillow. Please don't be afraid to ask for them.

THE VACUUM

The *vroom* of a Hoover may drive you nuts and cause you to miss a few phone calls, but it beats having a baby wailing directly into your eardrum. Some parents find this appliance so effective at quieting their child that they make a tape of the vacuum cleaner and play it several times a day like a Top 40 hit. Be forewarned, however, that some fussy babies are sensitive to loud sounds and will probably need some warning before the vacuum begins roaring away. Perhaps a running shower, the radio, or a lawn mower would make just the right prelude to a Domestic Concerto in V.

BLOW DRYER

The blow dryer operates under the same principles as the vacuum, only this device is a few very critical decibels lower. Blow dry the leaves of your alfalfa ferns after a good misting, or a freshly mopped floor, or your dog—anything—as long as it is near enough to your baby to purr her into serenity. If the blow dryer has a cool setting, you might try blowing her directly. Some kids adore wind sensations. However, never do this unless you've tested the temperature on yourself first.

WIND CHIMES

Chances are you'll get your money's worth with this calming instrument. The sounds of chimes, combined with the wind which generates them, can transfix practically any crying baby. Chimes with a more baritone sound are better than those higher pitched tones that sound like wine glasses clinking in a toast. This is a practical, not aesthetic, consideration; a crying baby won't be able to hear those soft sounds over her own ruckus. If weather prohibits you from rigging up some chimes outdoors, simply hang them from the ceiling, blow a fan in their direction, and cross your fingers.

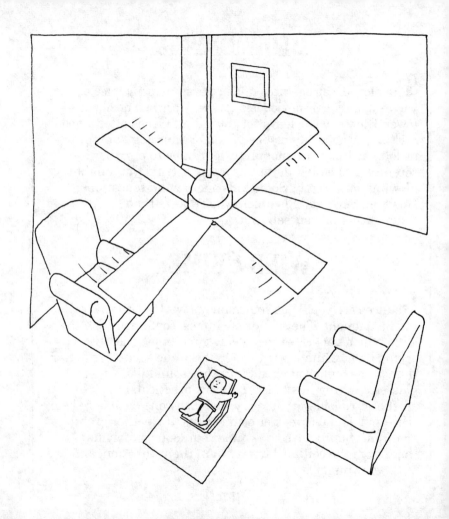

FANS

A window fan is a fantastic way to cool out a crying baby. Even if it's winter, set up your fan. Immediately. The purr and circular motion of a fan's blades can hypnotize most babies into a wide-eyed stare that is more amazed than amused. Most effective is low gear since it prevents the blades from dissolving into a big, uninteresting blur. Also, too much wind doesn't usually agree with babies.

Safety is a key concern with this method. Never, ever leave a child in reach of a fan. Better yet, use a ceiling fan, which is always out of harm's way. They are also useful in both hot and cold weather, meaning there's less explaining to do should some outsider come visit your home in February. Ceiling fans are big and unencumbered by any safety grates, providing more of a carousel-like show for baby to watch.

METRONOME

Metronomes are as good at quieting a baby as they are monotonous. Just set this musical beat-keeper at sixty or seventy beats per minute, wind it up, and let it tick away. It helps to place the metronome within view of baby since its metal stick flopping rhythmically back and forth enhances the metronome's quieting factor. This delightfully simple remedy sends many babies into a state of dulled quietude. The metronome is superior to the music box because once you wind it up, it ticks for up to forty-five minutes. Unfortunately, these items are not cheap. The least expensive portable costs at least $25. So, unless you fancy yourself a musician of sorts, or sense your child is the next Jascha Heifetz, you may want to borrow one and test its effectiveness first.

RATTLES

Rattles are great distractions. Just start shaking away with a rattle the minute your baby starts looking prunish. It's like a coach blowing his whistle, declaring interference. We always carried a rattle with us, in part because a good rattle is designed to be chewed. Babies can't cry and chew at the same time (or can they?).

111

WHISTLING

Like a referee at a basketball game, the trick here is to whistle the instant baby commits the foul of crying. For this solution to work, however, you must continue whistling beyond your first note. If you are like me and can't remember a complete version of anything except Happy Birthday and ninety-nine Bottles of Beer on the Wall, just move from song to song, creating medleys spontaneously, no thematic thread necessary. If you're stuck over what to spit out, Otis Redding's "Sitting on the Dock of the Bay" is an excellent standby.

SOUND SOLUTIONS

This solution is so innate you've probably discovered it already. Whispering "SHHHHH" into a baby's ear, over and over and over again, can actually work. It's highly doubtful he understands that the sound means to be quiet, but let's not quibble. It's important to fight back the inevitable urge to add two more letters to the "SHHH" sound. How would you feel if your child's first word was an obscenity?

Not to be too picayune, but it's important to avoid whispering "SHH" in a harsh or angry tone. It's a proven fact that a fussy child will not calm down when someone is delivering a teeth-gritting rendition of this sound solution. As a parent, you are destined to learn that one's tone of voice is often more important than the words themselves. So, take a few of those birthing breaths and begin a "SHHH" session that sounds more like a Hawaiian breeze than a fly with violent hiccups.

If you can roll your R's so that pronouncing Ricky Ricardo's name could take minutes to do, you come equipped with a great quieting sound. When baby begins slipping into a fretful state of mind, simply belt out a long trill. It works even better if you can add a high-pitched hum at the same time. There is something supremely distracting and mystifying about this birdlike sound. Repeat as often as necessary or until your lips feel as if they've been injected with Novocain.

AQUARIUM TANKS

Aquarium tanks emit just the right combination of bubbles, throaty hums, and mildly fluorescent light to captivate any baby. Colorful fish swimming about are an added bonus. Aquariums are perfect for bedrooms because their atmospheric calm is sleep inducing, and they make a terrific night light alternative to boot. However, before getting too excited by this option understand that there are two serious drawbacks: aquarium tanks are not cheap and they require upkeep. So, we suggest stopping by the pet shop or a friend's house first to test out your baby's reactions.

CAR WASH

Five minutes of industrial strength scrubs, suds, and slosh in a drive-through car wash is a perfect cry-stopper when baby gets fussy in the car. Car washing is such a completely amazing, thunderous event to any child that astonishment simply overwhelms any unhappiness. This solution can be cost-effective if you live or shop near a gas station offering free car washes when you buy a tank of gas. Hopefully, after a remedial trip to the car wash you'll leave with a happy baby, a clean car, and a definite sense of accomplishment.

WATER WORKS

COASTAL CURES

You and your baby don't need the sensitivity of a poet to enjoy the feeling of reprieve and relaxation offered by a walk along the ocean's shore. The steady, subtle sounds of waves, combined with salty air and wide open space, instantly cure fussing fits. If the weather is good and baby behaves as well as I predict, by all means, bring a blanket, a few toys, and a picnic to make a day of it. If she continues crying by the sea it's not a total loss; the ocean's blanketing sounds will all but drown her out.

WATERFALLS

The pounding of a waterfall and the bubbling brew below it stops most babies from crying (snap your fingers) "like that." If you're lucky enough to live near a waterfall, it's certainly worth the effort to go there. If, however, your baby fails to be silenced in the presence of one of nature's true wonders, just enjoy the fact that waterfalls muffle even Herculean cries, making them sound delightfully distant.

RIVER REMEDIES

The constant sound of a flowing river is a great fair-weather solution for the fussies. If you don't live near a river, you may consider taping the sounds to use at home or in the car. The sight of an ever-changing river is also quite settling to crying babies. And the fresh air of this outdoor expedition will certainly do you and baby some good.

FOUNTAINS

Whoever set the trend in shopping mall design had children, specifically fussy children, carved into the architectural plan. While your child is entranced by the spray of the inevitable water fountain, you can entertain yourself with a character study of Americana. I particularly like deciphering the expressions of those stray teenagers who hang around malls looking suspiciously intense. It helps to find a fountain with benches nearby so you can sit down on the job and let the magic of spewing water do all the work.

SPRINKLERS
The rhythmic sound of a rotating sprinkler can be as mesmerizing as a Handel symphony. Just park baby in a stroller while you water the lawn and watch her fussies dissolve into a somewhat hypnotic stupor. Meanwhile, parents are virtually off-duty. You must only play the role of supervisor, making sure to put stroller brakes on, park

the tot in a shaded area, and protect her from any un-
friendly stray dogs. If you have a back-yard picnic table,
sprinkling can become as much a part of dinnertime as
eating. It was for us, and our garden was never more moist.

THE LECTURE CIRCUIT

While this option is more preventive than interventive, it
provides you a much-needed opportunity to indulge your
mind and imagination in something beyond babyland.
Going to a lecture, movie, or concert can quiet a baby
simply by the stimulation of booming sounds, crowds of
people, and the vastness of a theater space. This solution
carries its risks, however. If dear baby emits those gurgling
sounds that, anywhere else, are so endearing, here they'll
be an unwelcomed distraction. A crying outburst is even
more problematic. Should any of these things happen,
smile, shake your head, and promptly exit.

For this reason, it is a good idea to plan your escape as
you would a fire drill. This avoids panic, confusion, and
minimizes ugly stares from the audience. Because there is
a good chance your outing will need to be aborted at some
point before the end, do not spend lots of money on tickets.
Despite these warnings, the benefits of a trip out on the
town far outweigh the risks.

CRACKLING FIRES

A roaring fire is a romantic solution to a most *un*romantic problem. Just as a fire's dancing flames and random crackles send adults into a relaxed, trancelike stare, the same usually holds true for babies, even the real fussers. An added benefit of crackling fires is their warmth, which helps soothe babies so effectively. All in all, this remedy is fairly effortless if you have three things working in your favor: a fireplace, a cold climate, and time. Time is important because when parking your baby before a roaring fire one must keep on constant guard, never leaving baby alone. In fact, it's best to hold him, so you can feel for yourself if the heat becomes too intense.

Miscellaneous,
or Everything Else,
Including

THE

KITCHEN

SINK

INVISIBLE ILLNESSES

Although it may sound morbid or even cruel to parents of those annoyingly perfect babies, it can be satisfying to discover that your baby's unhappiness is *caused* by something physical, something tangible, and best of all, something treatable.

Unbeknownst to most parents, particularly new ones, there are some illnesses undetectable by thermometer, diaper, or appetite. Topping this list of invisible illnesses is ear infection. Ear infection, according to the National Center for Health Statistics, is the most commonly found illness diagnosed during pediatric visits. Unlike most cases of colic, an ear infection will awaken a baby at night. Also, cold symptoms often accompany an ear infection, meaning running nose, low-grade fever, and watery eyes.

Urinary tract infections are also fairly common illnesses which are even harder to detect than an ear infection. They begin more slowly and subtly than an ear infection. It is recommended you ask your doctor to conduct urinalysis on your baby.

The best medical advice is this: make an appointment for your fussy baby to see a doctor. There is a slight chance a bona fide ailment is behind your baby's upset. And, if your baby checks out O.K., perhaps the doctor can give you advice and support for coping with your little hellion.

HERBAL SOLUTIONS

If you were one of those pregnant women who faithfully rubbed vitamin E along your expanding stomach and never touched caffeine—not even chocolate—then these herbal solutions are tailor-made for you and yours.

Herbal teas are most often recommended for "naturally" treating colicky behavior, the holistic way. One earth mother on my street claims a potion of cinnamon sticks, corn syrup, and warm water ended her daughter's grizzliness. Other folks proclaim the medicinal wonders of chamomile, catnip, fennel, and apple teas. Generally, these teas are given before feeding and are diluted heavily, about ten parts water to one part tea.

Caution is critical here because herbal remedies very often carry unhealthy side effects, despite their "all natural" labels. For example, senna, often found in teas like chamomile, is known to produce diarrhea (it is, in fact, considered an herbal laxative.) Do some research before using this solution. A medical or pharmacy school is a good place to find people trained in pharmacognosy, the study of natural herbs and plants, who can help you find the most effective and safest herbs for healing the high-maintenance baby.

THE COVER-UP

This simple game is a fantastic tear-stopper for babies over three months. Just put a scarf, towel, newspaper, or shirt (anything as long as it's soft and not dangerous) over your baby's head, wait a suspenseful thirty seconds (or less, if baby seems disturbed) while asking enthusiastically, "Where's my little darling?" and then whip off the cover and say excitedly, "Oh, *there* he is."

This peek-a-boo variation is a real kick for kids, even children as young as three or four months old. For parents, the cover-up demonstrates a baby's natural instinct to remove whatever is blocking his ability to breathe. Some people say this instinct helped produce the so-called "miracle babies" who survived the disastrous earthquake of 1985 in Mexico City. On the lighter side, though, exasperated parents with a strong imagination can pretend there is no baby during those few glorious seconds while baby is parked under a tunnel of darkness.

PERSONNEL PREFERENCES

It is astonishing and, depending on your mood, disconcerting to watch your hyperventilating baby turn into a Buddhist monk immediately upon entering the welcoming arms of another person. But, this does happen. As hard as it is to say, sometimes your baby is simply sick and tired of you.

If this is true, don't pout. Wallowing in self-pity and rejection robs you of the ability to enjoy the supreme freedom of time away from a fussy baby. Such personnel preferences are understandable if you think about yourself. Certainly you have a friend, relative, or spouse you love and usually love to be with *except* on those certain occasions when you'd rather spend time stuck in a revolving door than with him or her. Everyone has limits—even babies.

Mothers, especially, can feel victimized by personnel preferences due to a certain injustice dealt by nature. It is often *only* around mothers that babies cry. It's hard to accept that the child who is so happily entertained with his blocks and stuffed animals will begin to fuss the moment you walk into the room. According to experts, this annoying stage sets in during the last three months of the first year. And, rumor has it that this phase lasts through the college years.

VISUAL AIDS

Posters, Pop Art, flags, Navajo rugs, even Hi-C cans and striped shirts all fall into that open-ended category of visual aids. Taking your grimacing infant on a tour of local colorful objects—including a trip through your refrigerator—usually distracts him into a state of studious quietude. Be prepared to show many items, if necessary, many times a day. Museums, art galleries, mall corridors, university art department hallways almost always offer an entertaining array of visual aids if you're in the mood to explore beyond the confines of your home.

TV WATCHING

I'll admit it—it's shameful to include television watching. We've all, no doubt, heard experts warn that parking your child in front of the tube breeds passive, nonthinking clones of American marketing and Hollywood sensibilities. However, I would be robbing you of a handy device if I failed to mention that turning on the television stills many high-need babies. Television watching isn't called escapist for nothing—it keeps discomforts and dissatisfaction away on a thirty-minute by thirty-minute basis.

Animal shows are tops, but little ones are indiscriminate. Babies have been known to love shows ranging from "Wheel of Fortune" to bowling to "Sesame Street." Some baby experts say just the whining sound of a station off the air along with the static picture quiets a fussy baby wonderfully. That solution, however, can seem especially desperate and sad. A word of caution here: This can turn on you when your child becomes verbal and demands TV after every meal. Use this device sparingly.

PRINTED MATTER

Even the fussiest of babies will gaze into a page of Mother Goose, *National Geographic,* or *Glamour* as contentedly as a bookworm at the New York City Public Library. The trick here is to keep those colorful pages coming. Avoid anything without pictures; *Foreign Affairs* must wait until nap time. Always arrive armed with a pile of books, magazines, even photo albums. You'd be surprised how quickly you can flip through a month of *New Yorkers* when pictures, including advertisements, are the sole pursuit.

Books and magazines are excellent travel mates. Many subway rides for us entailed plenty of oinking, buzzing and

meowing along with a favorite animal book to stave off a potentially debilitating scene in public (scenes always seem worse when there's an audience). At certain stages in your baby's life it makes good health and economic sense to buy books that are as readable as they are chewable.

THE GREAT OUTDOORS

All babies are part angel, part comedian, part monster, and part Yule Gibbons. Getting fresh air into your baby's overworked lungs can be as settling as walking out of an Iron Maiden heavy-metal rock concert.

Before launching into a more elaborate quieting method, try walking outside first. If you hear the sounds of birds chirping or traffic moving along nearby streets, consider this method a success. To hear *anything* other than crying means your baby is no longer drilling holes through your abused eardrums.

Foul weather is no excuse for bypassing this recommendation. Think creatively and don't treat your baby like a wimp, overprotecting her from inclement weather. Take heed of this fact: Many babies born in Finland sleep outside, bundled up, based on the accepted cultural assumption that fresh air builds a sturdier constitution.

BABY WATCHING

Narcissism begins in the crib. Proof of this statement lies in all the mirrors shimmering on rattles, pop-up toys, and the standard crib-side companion, the Activity Center. Babies love watching themselves. Although it takes a while for baby to realize she is watching herself, the pleasure of staring eye-to-eye is engaging nonetheless. Our daughter now greets the mirror with a super friendly "Hi" when bumping into herself while on an infamous search-and-destroy mission through the house.

When using this quieting method, it is imperative to begin before a flood of tears does. Baby watching is ineffective with blurred vision. This is a tactic which falls under the category of quick fixes. No matter how narcissistic, staring at oneself grows dull pretty fast— unless, of course, you're George Hamilton or Elizabeth Taylor.

If your whiz kid doesn't notice herself in the mirror, tap on the glass a few times.

CREATURE COMFORTS

If you don't own a dog or cat or cow, for that matter, you must either buy, steal, borrow, or visit one. Animals are all but guaranteed to calm babies. For some inexplicable reason children instinctively adore creatures with two eyes, a nose, and mouth that aren't their parents.

We got a kitten from the pound to help us baby-sit. The cat has proved to be a handy distraction that has a tremendous tolerance for abuse. The way our daughter treats this cat makes me fear the day a new baby enters Godzilla's domain. One advantage about cats is that they are relatively maintenance free.

Many parents understandably feel overwhelmed at the thought of another needy creature, demanding to be fed, cleaned up after, and loved. If this is your reaction, visit the

nearby zoo or farm or ask a neighbor if their dog is available for house calls. Don't be bashful.

O.K.–true confessions. I got so desperate at times that I used to stop my daughter from crying during strolls through the neighborhood by saying, "Hey, look at the dog. See the doggie?" She'd forget all discomforts as quickly as any lottery winner and start madly searching around for the phantom dog. She became infinitely happier just by the expectation that a bouncing, huffing, hairy canine would bring some life to the too familiar streets, rubbed duller with every new track laid by our Graco stroller. Sometimes I'd get lucky and a stray dog would walk our way. However, this didn't happen enough to ease the guilt I felt from this untruth. But, hey, I stopped my child from irritating me and waking up the neighbors and that seemed justification enough at the time.

THE KITCHEN SINK

It's mundane, it's absurd, it's wasteful, but good Lord is it ever terrific at snuffing out a crying fit. Turning on a faucet is a down-and-dirty survival trick for you and your crying baby. Like many solutions touted in these pages, I happened upon this one quite by accident. One day while brushing my teeth, crying child on hip, the kid suddenly shut up. I turned off the water. . .the crying resumed. I turned on the water. . .the crying stopped. Needless to say, pretty soon my daughter and I were holding late-night vigils by the kitchen sink. Here in the desert of Arizona water is truly a precious resource, but my environmental consciousness went down the drain—so to speak—when faced with such a domestic crisis. It's a good idea to hold baby within view of the running faucet. This is truly where a Zen mind comes in handy, because what is there to do as you hold a baby in front of a running faucet but meditate, or moan.